MORE DINOSAURS!

AND OTHER PREHISTORIC BEASTS

MORE
DINOSAURS!
AND OTHER PREHISTORIC BEASTS

A DRAWING BOOK
BY
Michael Emberley

Little, Brown and Company
Boston   Toronto

Third Printing

Library of Congress Cataloging in Publication Data

Emberley, Michael.
  More dinosaurs!

  Summary: Provides patterns for drawings of the
longisquama, protoceratops, woolly mammoth, and nine
other prehistoric animals, based on the evidence of
fossil remains.
    1. Dinosaurs in art — Juvenile literature. 2. Extinct
animals in art — Juvenile literature. 3. Animal painting
and illustration — Juvenile literature. [1. Dinosaurs
in art. 2. Prehistoric animals in art. 3. Animal
painting and illustration. 4. Drawing books] I. Title.
NC780.5.E42 1983   743'.6   83-9822
ISBN 0-316-23424-9

                    WOR

*Published simultaneously in Canada
by Little, Brown & Company (Canada) Limited*

PRINTED IN THE UNITED STATES OF AMERICA

CONTENTS

What, Where, How...

This row shows what to draw.

This row shows where to draw it.

All the animals in this book, no matter how complicated they seem, are made up of these simple, easy-to-draw shapes.

Each shape does not have to be drawn perfectly; you do not need a compass or a ruler. Slightly crooked lines will do just fine. ∿ means add color.

Protoceratops

(pro-to-SER-a-tops)
"early horned-face"
6 feet long

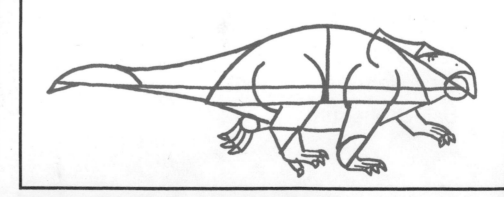

Etc.

Since no one has ever seen a living dinosaur, or any other prehistoric beast, you can color your drawings any way you want.

THIS IS THE ANIMAL'S NAME.
THIS IS HOW TO SAY IT.
THIS IS WHAT IT MEANS.
THIS IS HOW BIG IT WAS.

You can use the big pictures for coloring ideas, or you can just use your imagination. The drawings for this book were made with felt-tip pens; however, you can use pencil, crayon, paint, or anything else you have.

7

Longisquama

(long-is-QUA-ma)

"long scaled"

4 feet long

9

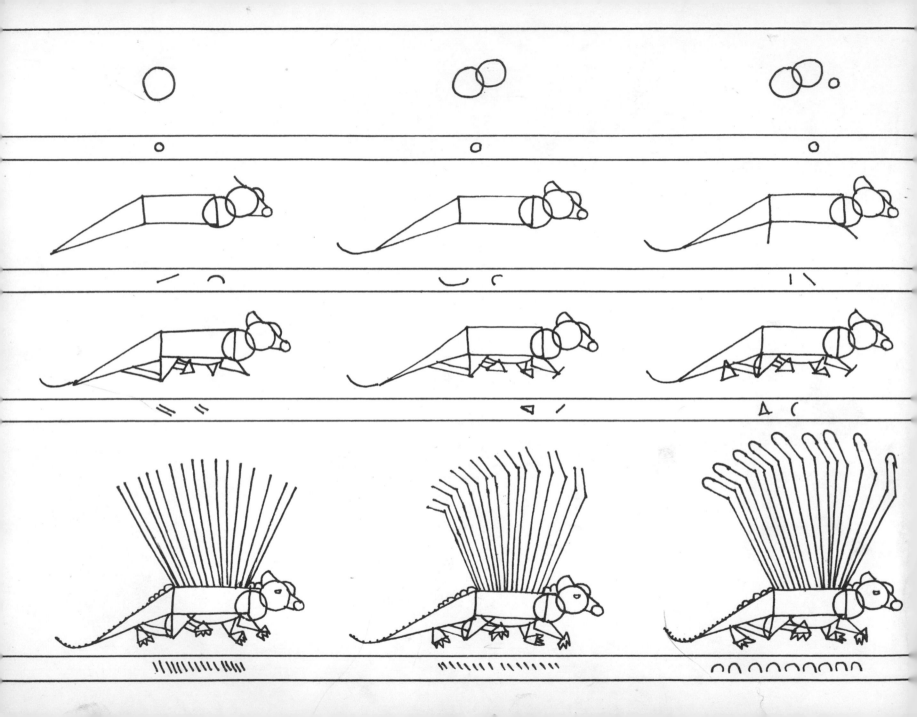

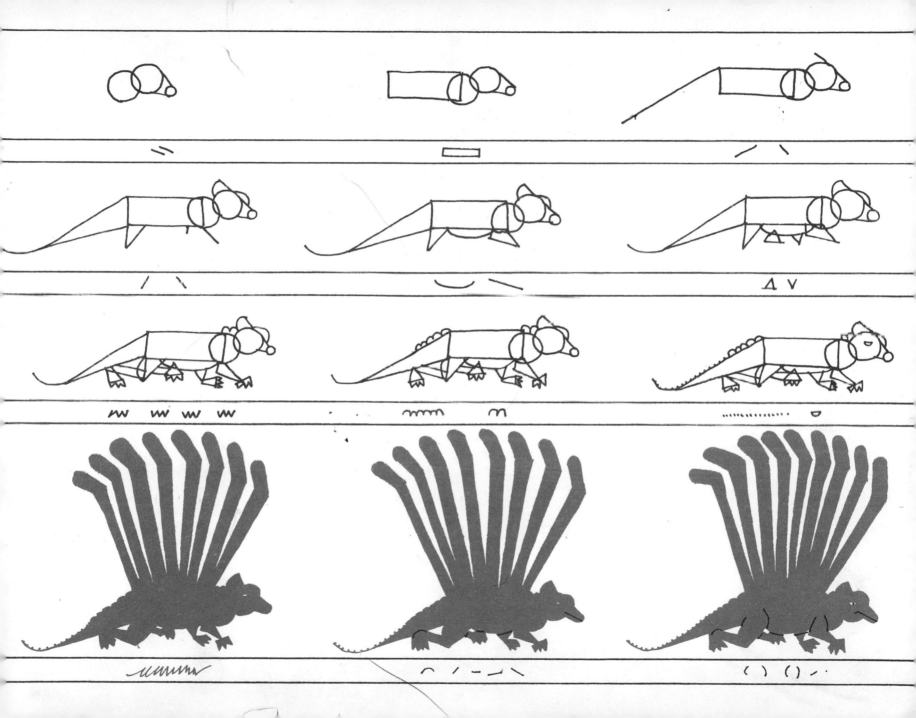

Protoceratops

(pro-to-SER-a-tops)
"early horned-face"
6 feet long

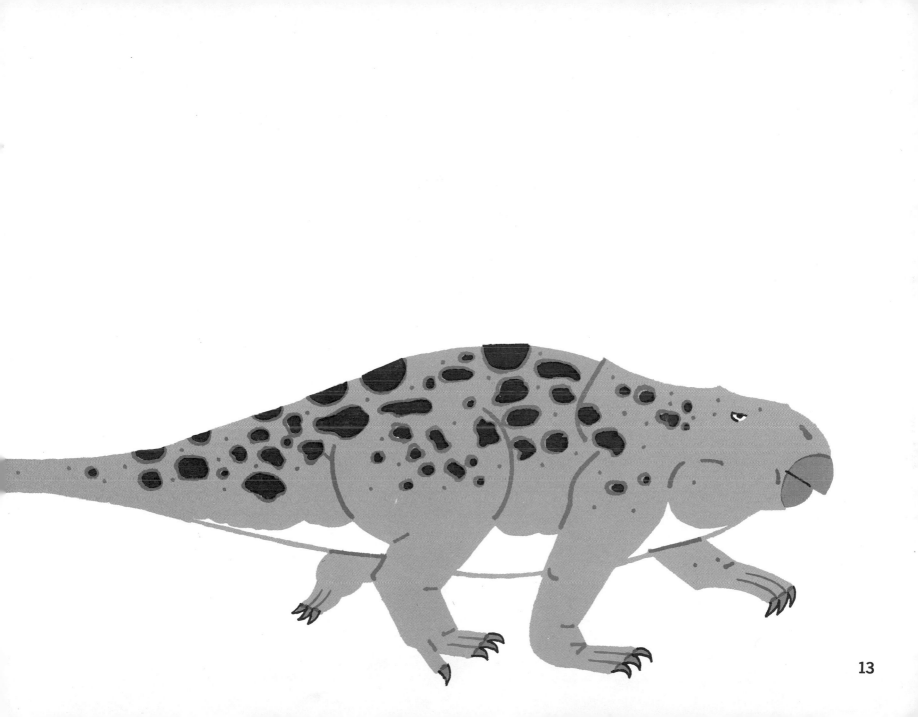

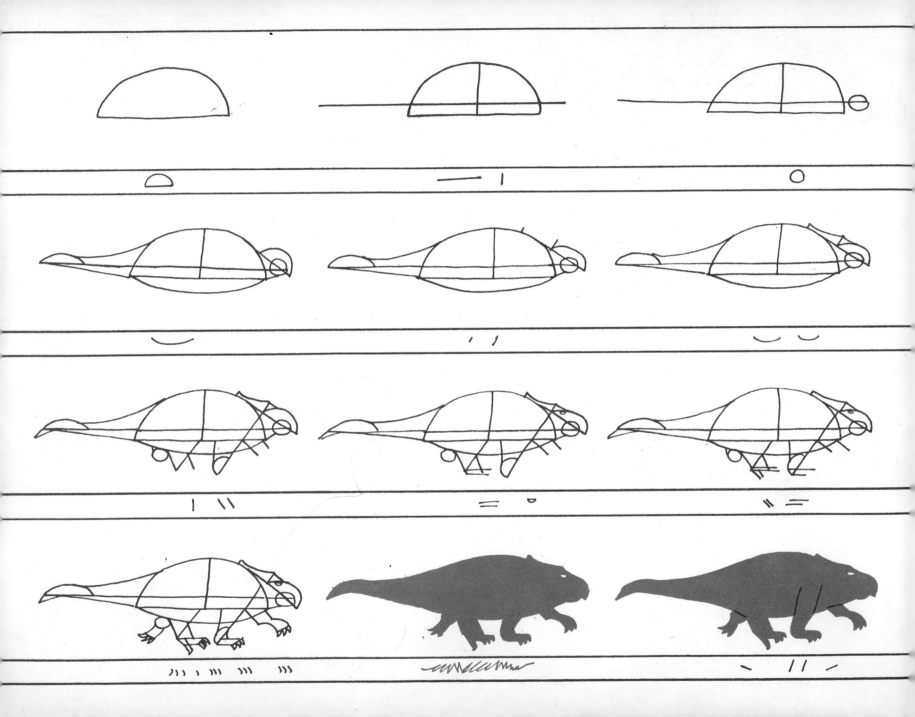

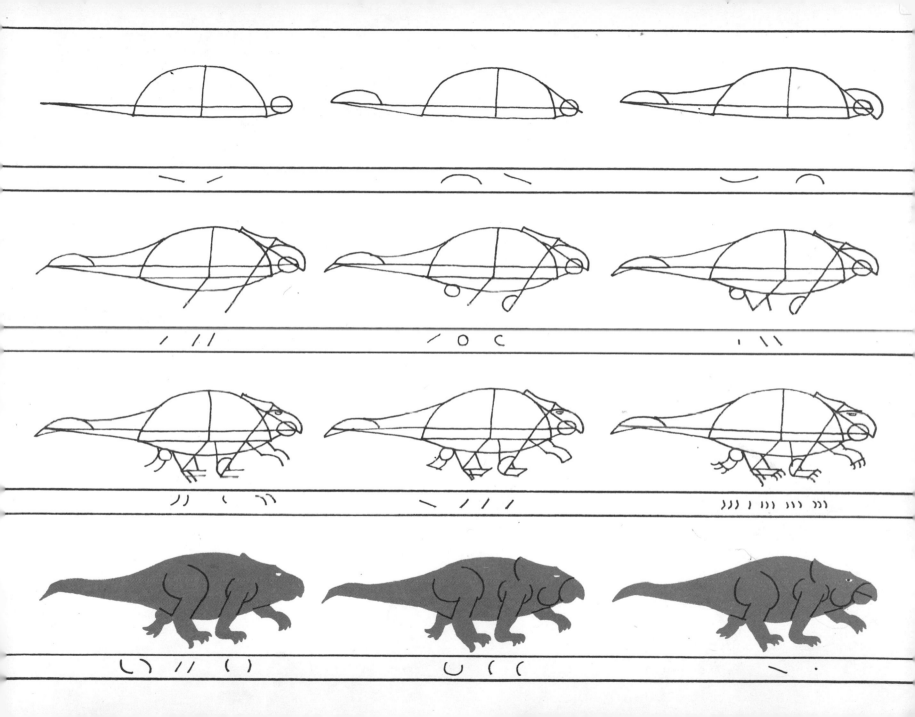

Dinichthys

(dye-NICK-this)
"terrible fish"
35 feet long

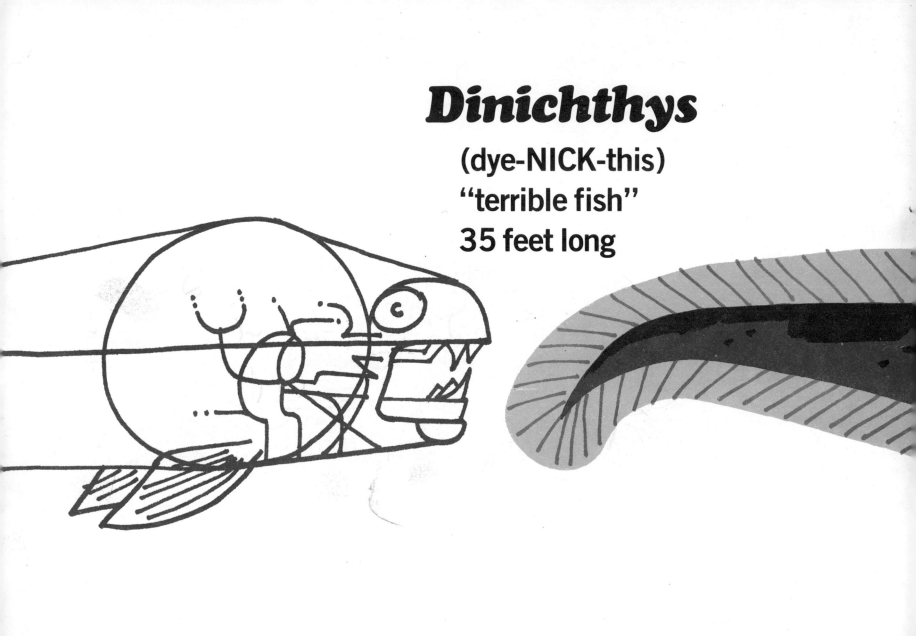

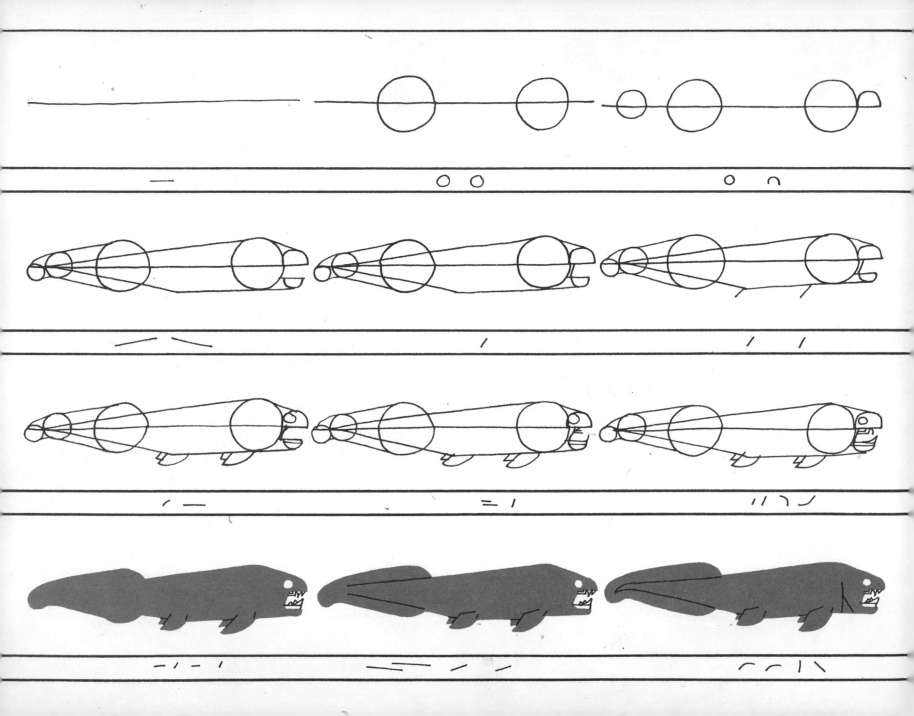

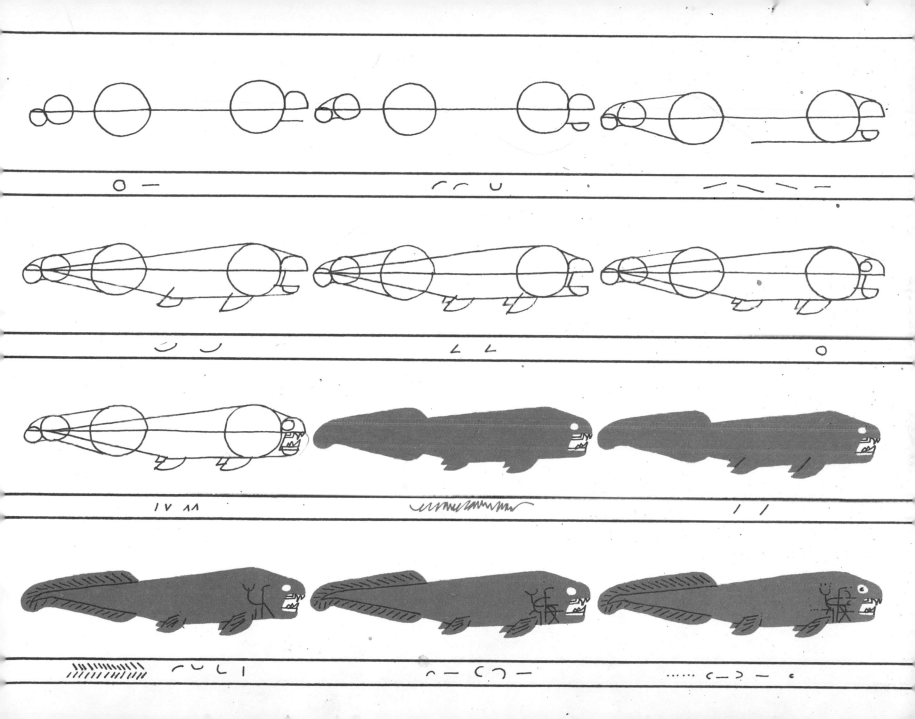

Dimorphodon

(dye-MOR-fo-don)
"two forms of teeth"
6-foot wingspan

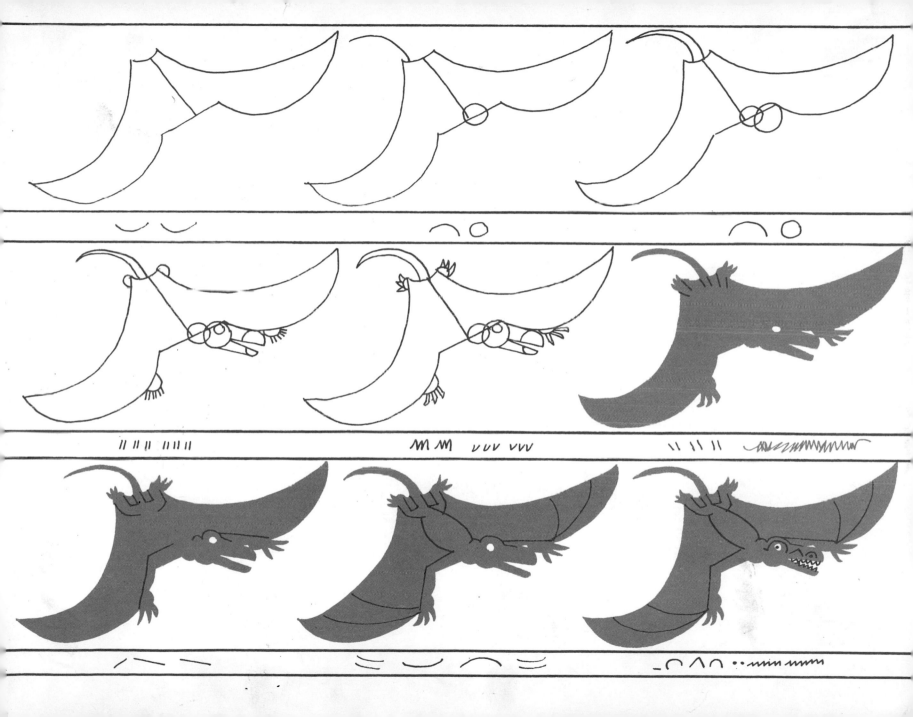

Ceratogaulus

(sair-a-to-GAW-lus)
"horned digger"
2 feet long

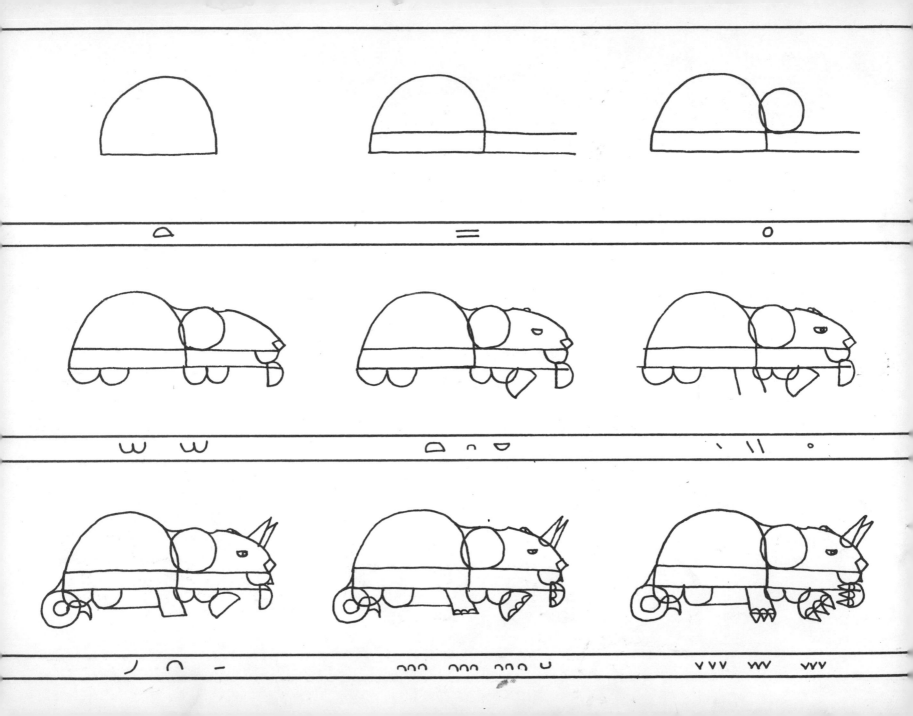

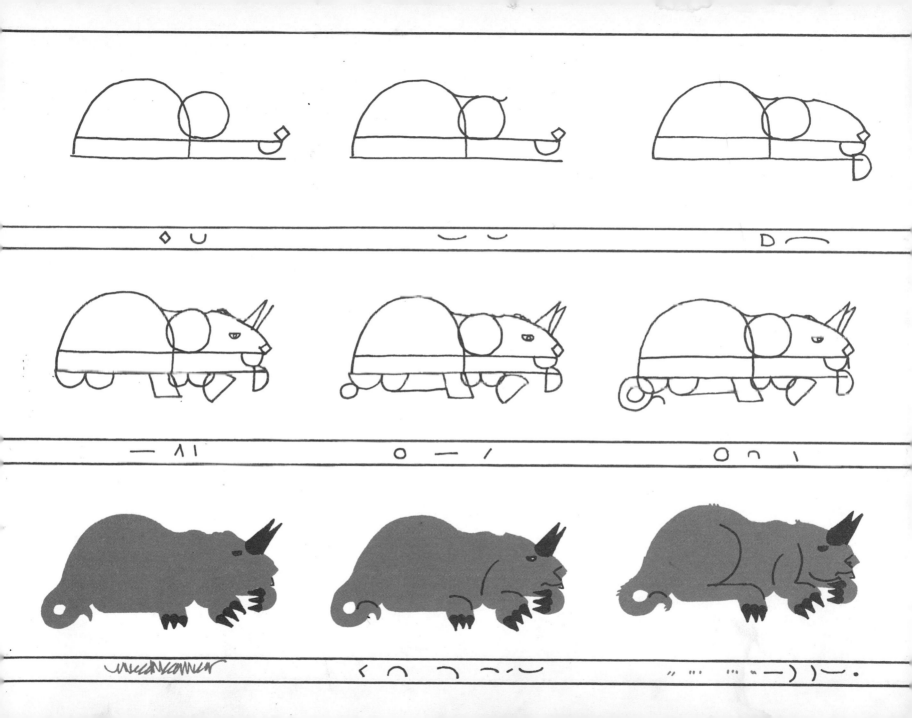

Zeuglodon

(ZOO-glow-don)
"strap tooth"
60 feet long

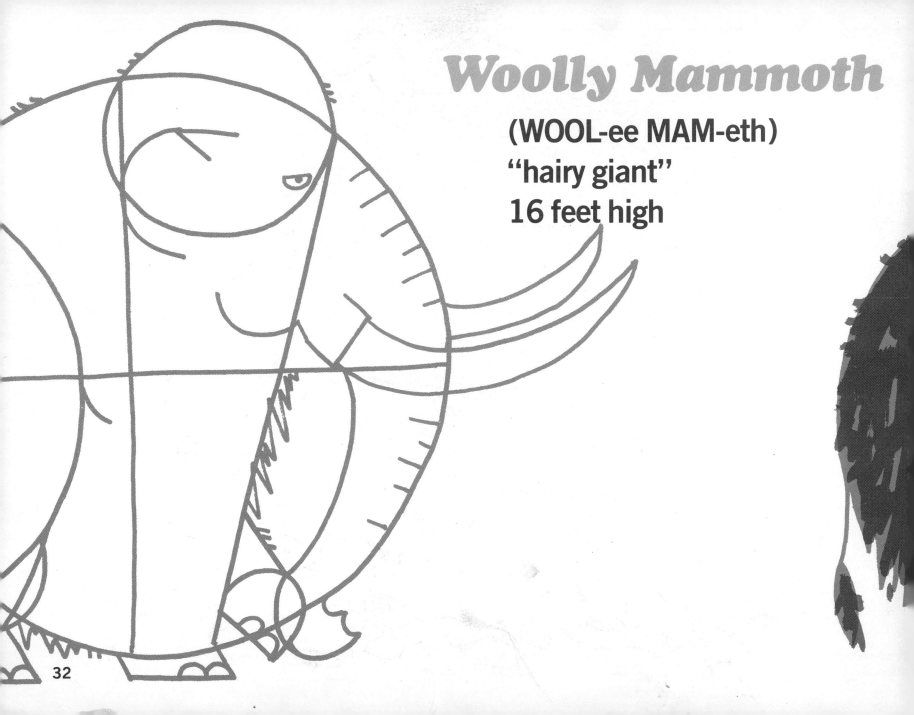

Woolly Mammoth

(WOOL-ee MAM-eth)
"hairy giant"
16 feet high

Tylosaurus

(tye-lo-SAW-rus)
"knot lizard"
30 feet long

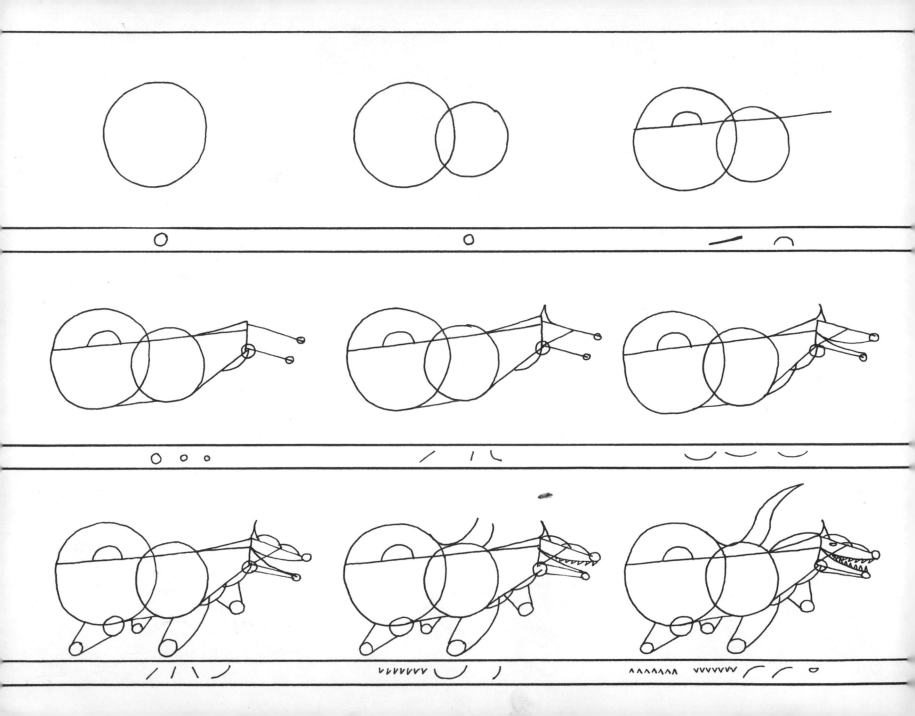

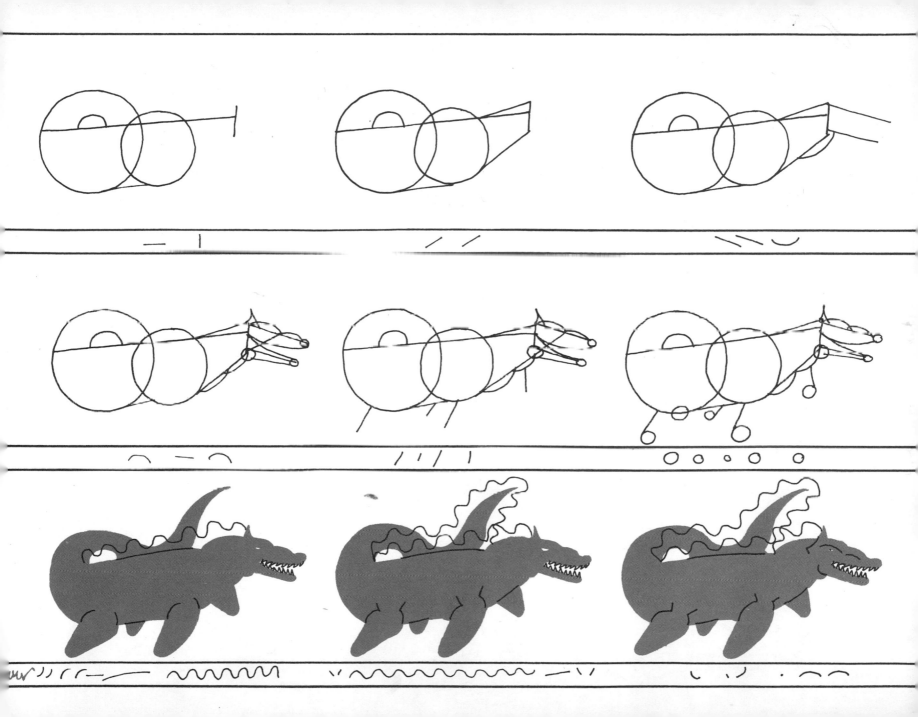

Glyptodont

(GLIP-to-dont)

"grooved tooth"

10 feet long

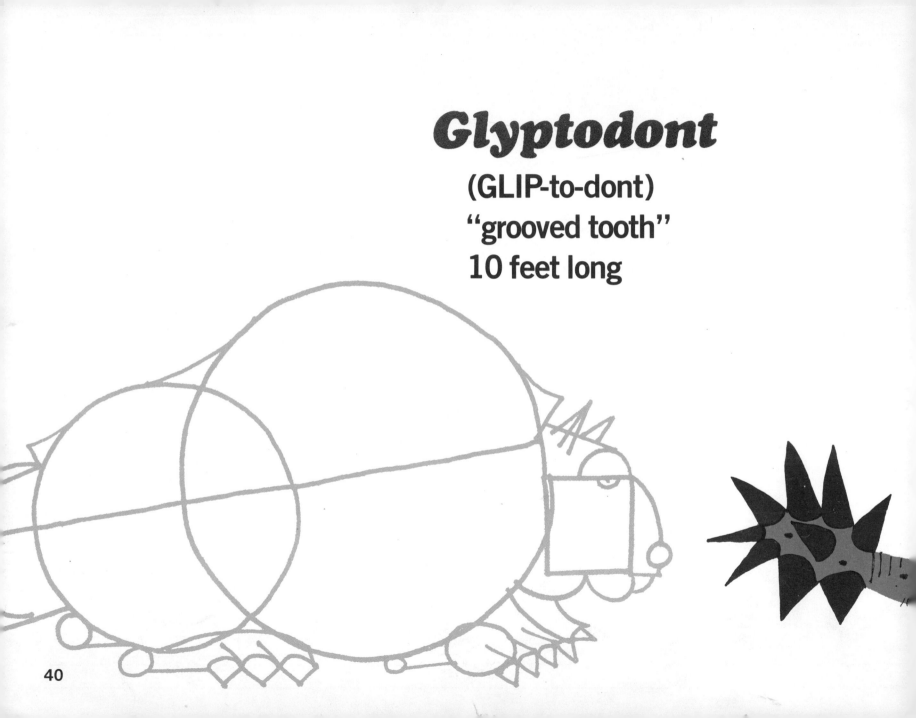

41

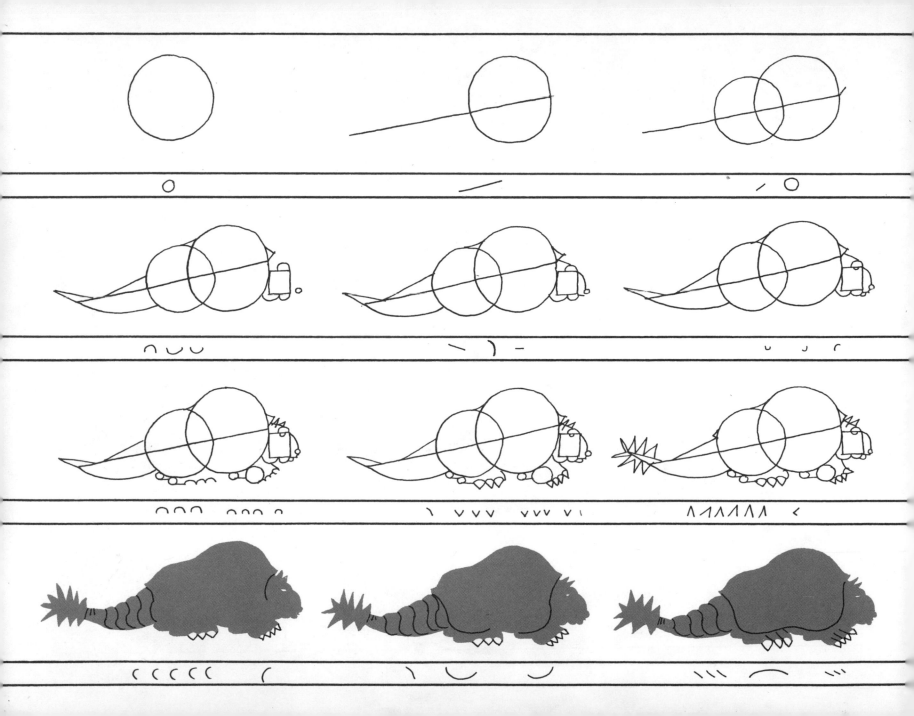

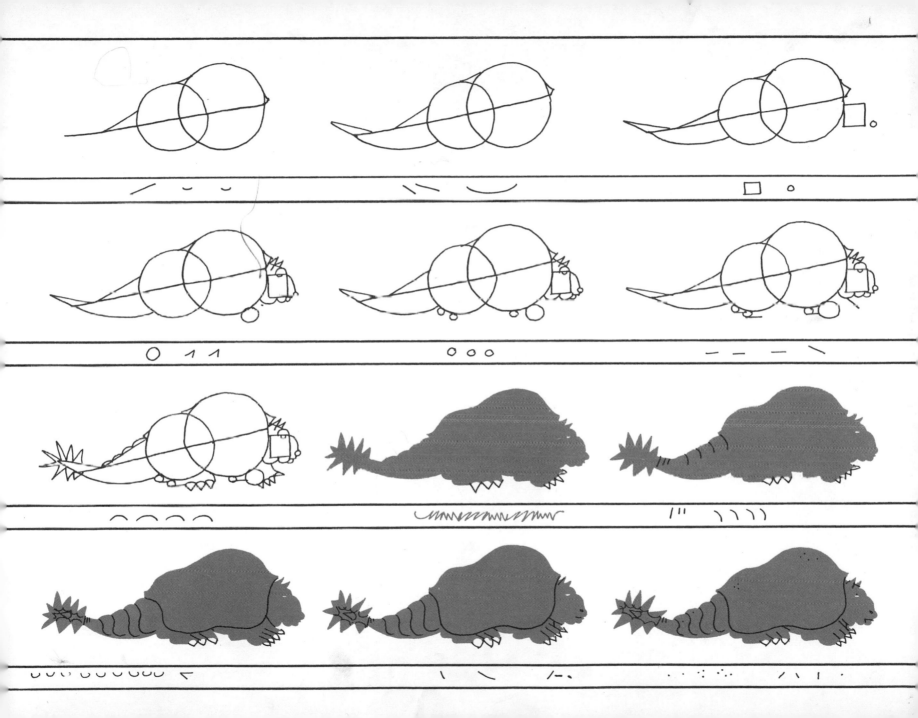

Archaeopteryx

(ar-key-OP-ter-icks)
"ancient wing"
18 inches long

45

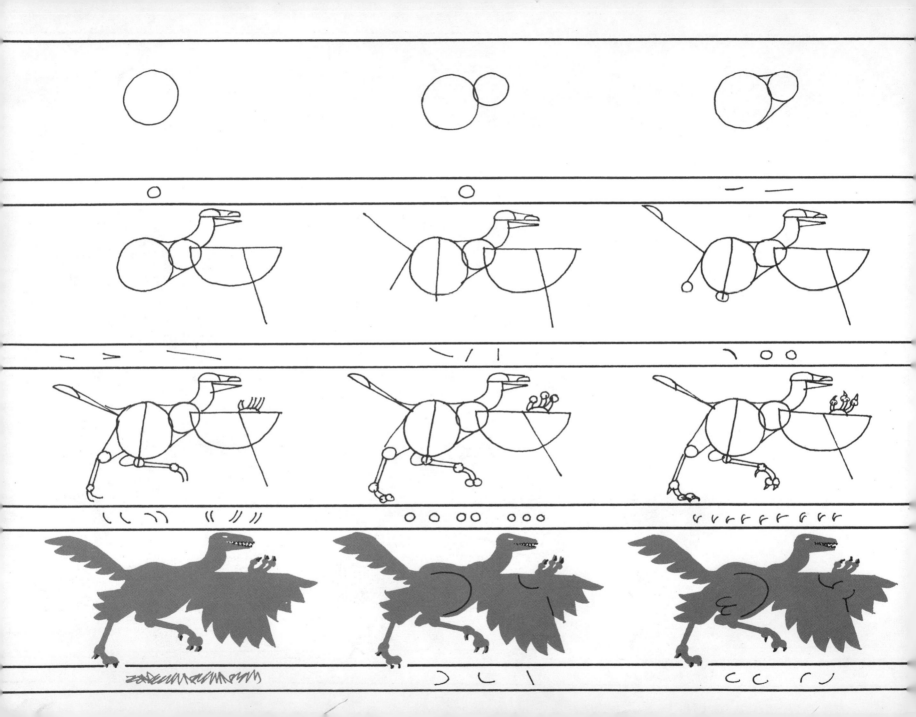

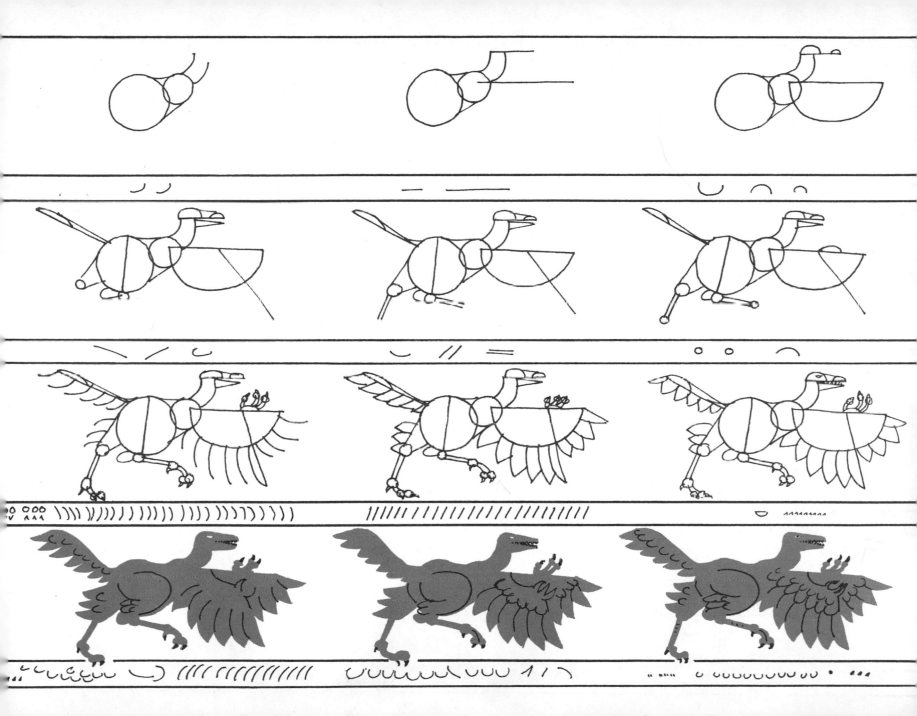

Smilodon

(SMILE-o-don)
"carving-knife tooth"
10 feet long

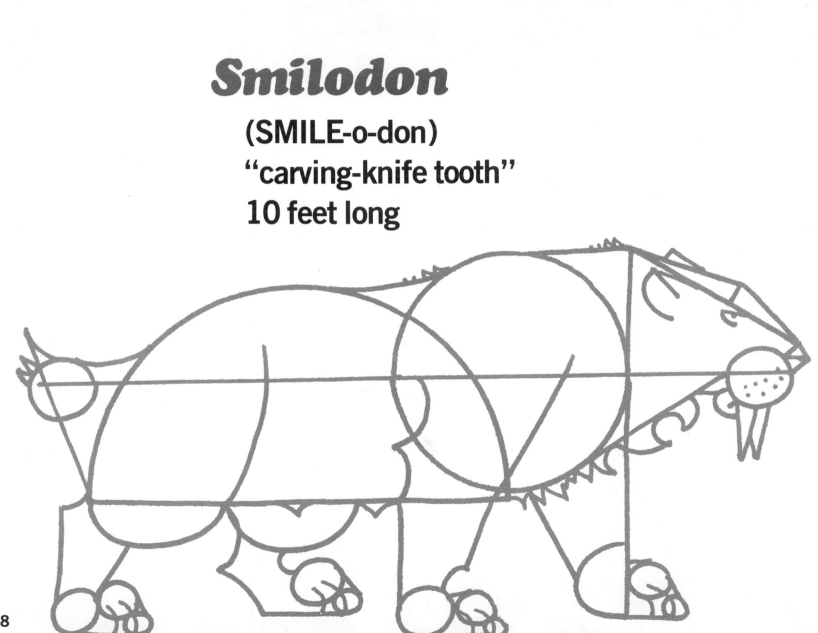

49

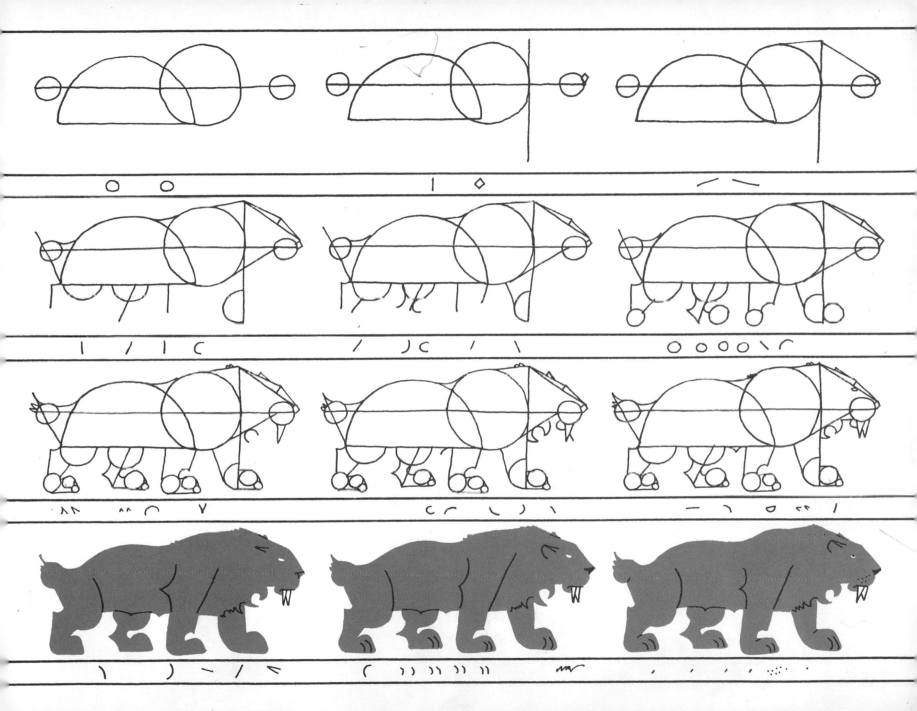

Baluchitherium

(bah-luke-i-THEE-ree-um)
"beast from Baluchistan"
18 feet high

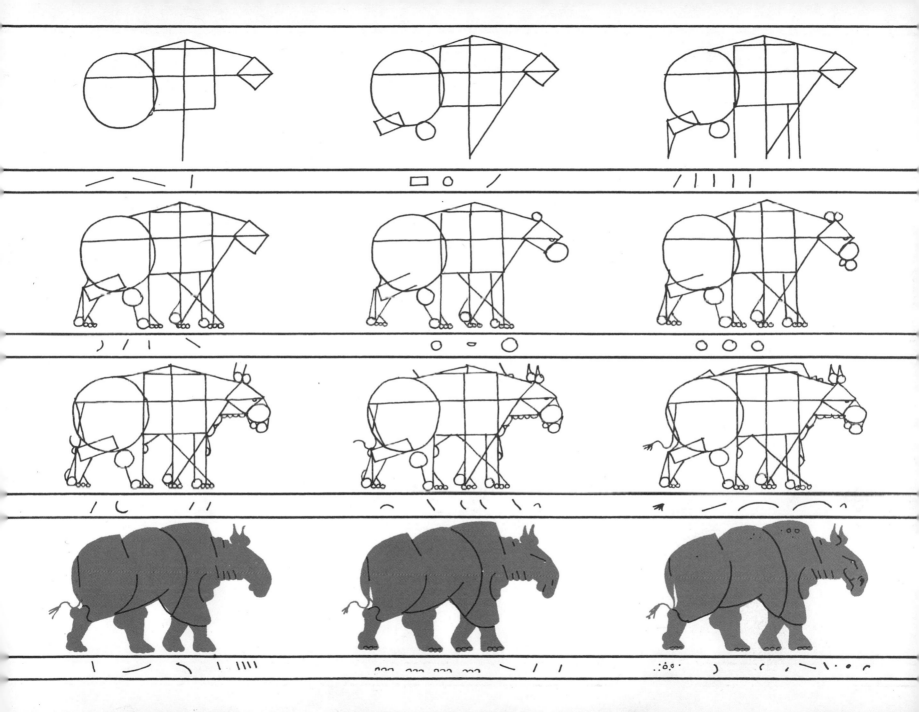

None of the animals in this book are alive today, but scientists can tell what they were like by studying the preserved impressions of their bones, which are called fossils. By comparing these fossils to the bones of living animals, scientists can get a good idea of what prehistoric animals looked like. Some of these animals have been easier to figure out than others. For instance, Zeuglodon bones were much like modern whale bones. Scientists were able to reconstruct the beast using what they have learned about whale anatomy.

Zeuglodon, Smilodon, Glyptodont, Baluchitherium, and Ceratogaulus are all mammals. They lived between 10 and 50 million years ago. The Woolly Mammoth is also a mammal, but it lived only 1 million years ago, about the time that another mammal, man, was beginning to emerge.